Against a background of enormous political turmoil and two unfortunate marriages, King Carol II of Romania's relationship with the flame-haired Magda Lupescu was to remain a constant source of comfort to him. For the love of Magda, he twice went into exile and finally gave up his kingdom. For her part, she followed her lover halfway round the world and was still at his side as friend and confidante after nearly 30 years.

♕ *The young Prince was the first child of Crown Princess Marie, herself just 18 years old, above*

SUNDAY'S CHILD

AS SOON AS THE CROWN PRINCE OF ROMANIA REACHED MARRIAGEABLE AGE, THE SEARCH WAS ON FOR A SUITABLE BRIDE BUT CAROL HAD PLANS OF HIS OWN. MEANWHILE, A FLIRTATIOUS ADVENTURESS WAS BECOMING THE TALK OF HER HOME TOWN

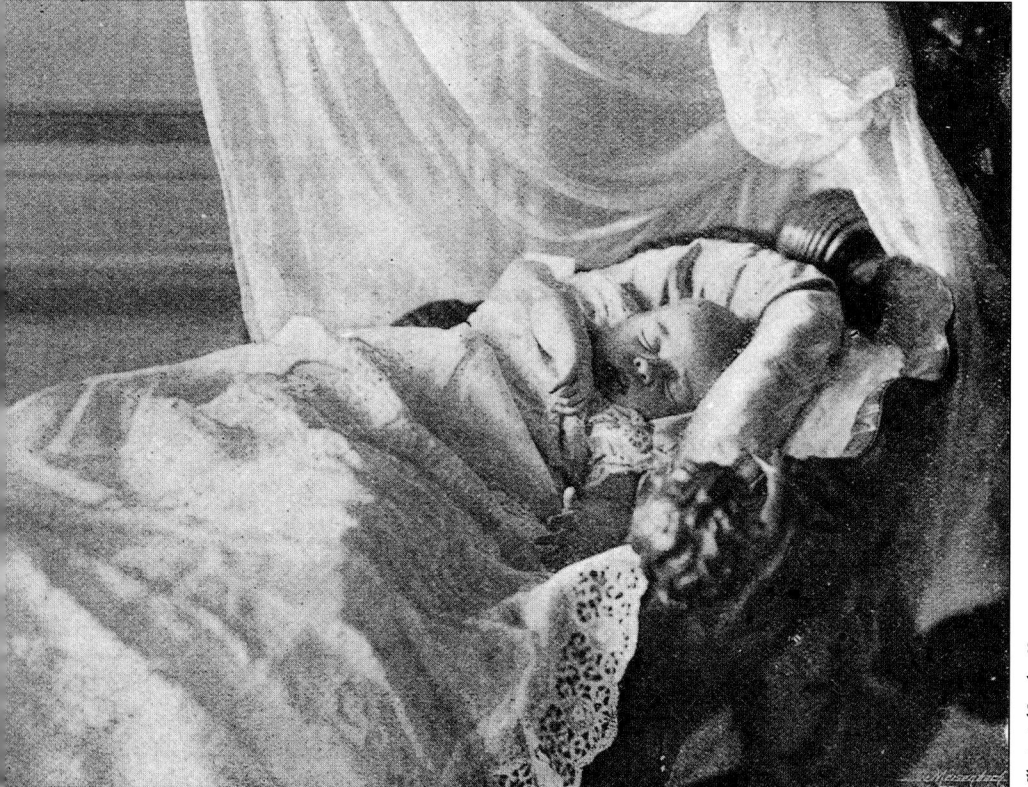

♕ *The birth of the baby Carol, Crown Prince of Romania, was greeted by the firing of 101 cannons. His life was not to be as peaceful as these early slumbers*

♕ *Three generations of Romanian royals, far right, in the grounds of Castle Peles. From left, future King Ferdinand, Princess Elisabetha, Queen Elisabeth, Crown Prince Carol, his mother Marie, Prince Nicolas and Carol I*

C arol, Crown Prince of Romania, was born at Castle Peles, in the Carpathian Mountains, on Sunday, 15 October 1893. It was the first time that the birth of a royal heir had taken place in the country, and 101 cannons saluted the great event. The baby's mother, Crown Princess Marie, had just celebrated her 18th birthday, and she was thrilled with her 'big, healthy and exceedingly amiable baby.'

It was not always easy for Marie to take care of her son as she would have liked. For although he grew up in a highly privileged world, he was surrounded by larger-than-life figures, who were constantly jockeying for position. Thanks to their machinations, Carol developed a sense of insecurity not even his doting mother could dispel.

King Carol I

The most dominant personalities of Carol's childhood were his great uncle and aunt, King Carol I and Queen Elisabeth.

Romania's royal dynasty was a German implant that had taken root shortly after the country gained independence from the Turks in the 1860s. King Carol I feared anarchy on all sides and ruled both his people and his family with true Prussian rigidity.

The Queen could hardly have been more different. She was a poetess, writing under the pseudonym of Carmen Sylva, who presided over an adoring circle of artists and intellectuals and encouraged 'mystic' experiences. She lived up to her part by wearing diaphanous white dresses, with her long hair cascading over her shoulders.

Queen Elisabeth alternately spoiled Carol and ignored him, while her husband was uniformly severe in his treatment of all prospective heirs to the throne. Carol I allowed Marie no say in her children's education and she got little support from her husband, the shy, weak Ferdinand, when she asked him to intervene.

Queen Victoria's granddaughter

Carol's mother was the daughter of Alfred, Duke of Edinburgh (Queen Victoria's son) and the Grand Duchess Marie of Russia. Spirited and beautiful, she was used to speaking her mind freely. A fervent lover of the open air, she found the atmosphere in the Bucharest palace terribly stifling, and Ferdinand was no match for her.

👑 *Crown Prince Carol nursing his younger brother Nicolas*, below. *It was the Prince's military bearing – as well as his shiny black boots, right – that were to win the heart of a young girl who would one day become his wife*

Popperfoto

After Carol, Marie had five more children: two sons (Nicolas and Mircea) and three daughters (Elisabetha, Marie and Ileana). All of them survived into adulthood, except for the younger boy, Mircea, who died in 1916 of typhoid when just three years old.

The Romanians loved to gossip about their sovereigns' private lives, especially if there was a hint of sexual scandal in the air. People said that baby Mircea's real father was Baron Barbu Stirbey, Marie's most faithful confidant, whom she had met in 1907. Stirbey was related to the most powerful statesmen in Romania and he was to become the bane of Carol's life.

It was also common knowledge that Ferdinand had fallen deeply in love with a Romanian girl, Helena Vacarescu, before his marriage to Marie. King Carol had forbidden this romance because of an unwritten rule that members of the royal family could not marry Romanian nationals. This taboo was to dog the young Carol in the unhappy years to come and it eventually entered Romanian law in the 1920s.

Childhood years

During his childhood, Carol's home alternated between Castle Peles and the cavernous Cotroceni Palace in Bucharest. He was brought up by a series of governesses and private tutors, who were generally engaged by his great uncle, King Carol I. His mother was never consulted on the matter, with the result that she detested most of them and suspected them of trying to turn the child Carol against her.

At the age of 11, all Carol cared about was being a soldier. He liked books about the army and was a great admirer of the precision of military life. According to Marie, he was a stickler for things being done properly, and there was no sign, as yet, of the man whose name was to hit newspaper headlines as a notorious womaniser.

But he had already made an impression on one small girl. Ioana Lambrino was five years old when she first met Carol at a charity gala in Bucharest. Carol was 11, and appeared wearing a military uniform and big, black, shiny boots. Ioana, better known by her nickname of 'Zizi', recalled in her memoirs that she thought Carol's footwear 'the highest possible form of elegance.'

When he was 19, Carol was sent to the military academy in Potsdam, Germany, where he

Süddeutscher Verlag Bilderdienst

👑 *Carol attended the military academy at Potsdam in Germany, where he and his father were photographed*, above, *during 1914*

Illustrated London News

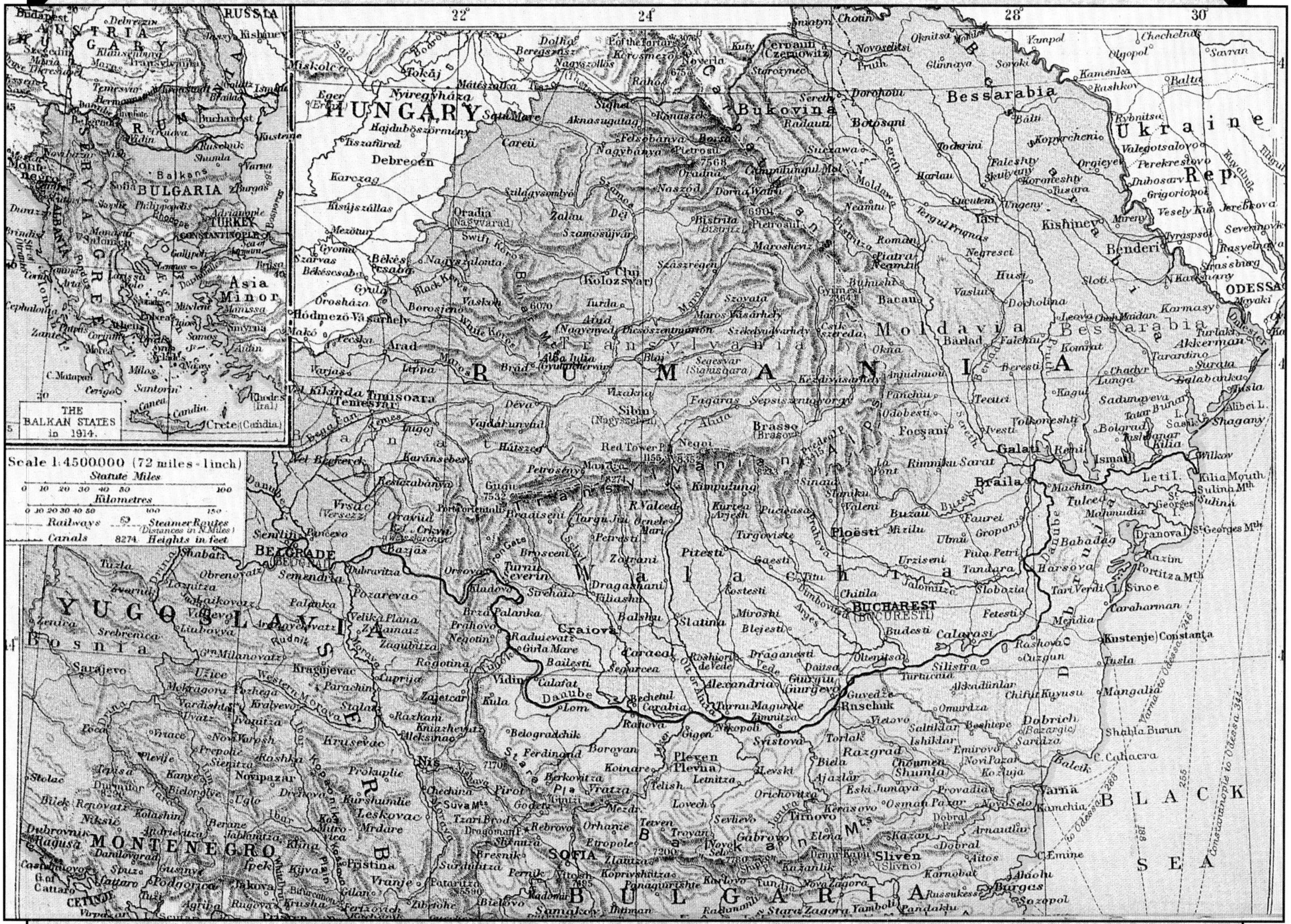

Ray Duns

ROMANIA: A YOUNG NATION AND AN ANCIENT PEOPLE

Romania (normally spelt 'Rumania' in the years between the World Wars) was once an outpost of Imperial Rome, and its inhabitants claimed descent from the colonists of that time. For 400 years, the land was under Turkish rule, but became independent in 1862, being given a German King in 1866.

As well as having very fertile land, the region is also rich in minerals – including oil, of which Romania was once the main source in Europe. The climate varies widely, with hot, Mediterranean summers but harsh winters, during which the Danube, the chief waterway, is frozen for three months.

Under the terms of the Treaty of Versailles following World War 1, the country was granted extra territories which almost doubled its size and population (to about 17 million, of whom in Carol's day most were peasant farmworkers). As well as Romanian, the educated classes also spoke French, but the people included descendants of many races. Apart from politics, most were united by the Greek Orthodox Church, although five per cent were Jewish – at that time, the largest proportion of any country in the world.

Hulton-Deutsch Collection

Popperfoto

joined his father's old regiment. Surprisingly, this was his mother's idea, and Carol, free at last from the constraints and intrigue of palace life, was extremely happy in the military school's ordered environment.

Marriageable age

Over six feet tall and slim, with lively, dark blue eyes and fair hair, Carol had grown into a good-looking young man. Now that he was of marriageable age, Ferdinand and Marie set about looking for a suitable bride for Carol and eventually settled on the Grand Duchess Olga, eldest daughter of Tsar Nicholas and Tsarina Alexandra of Russia. But although they tried hard to foster a courtship, neither Carol nor Olga was interested. In any case, Carol had quite different plans.

Romania took a neutral position in the first two years of the 1914-18 war, but in 1916, promised large territories by the Entente nations of Britain, France and Russia, she attacked Austria-Hungary. Although he was technically on active service, as royal heir, Carol was forbidden to fight and he stayed well behind the battle lines until late in the war, indulging his passions for smart cars and aeroplanes.

In love with Zizi

Casting his eyes around the pretty girls of Bucharest, he fell for one called Ella Filitti, and when she was sent out of the country as a result of his infatuation, he quickly turned to the sister of a childhood friend. This was none other than Zizi Lambrino, who had so admired his dashing figure in 1904. By the time Carol was supposed to be cultivating Olga, he had fallen deeply in love and determined to make Zizi his wife.

One of the myths created from the first of Carol's great love affairs was that Zizi was a gypsy dancer. She was, in fact, related by marriage to Prince Alexander Cuza and her family was often received at court. But she was Romanian and a commoner and, as such, it was out of the question that Carol should marry her.

During the war, their friendship had gone virtually unnoticed at the palace and the news came as a complete surprise to his parents. So when he announced his intentions at a family dinner party, his news was greeted in total silence while Ferdinand slowly stroked his beard and Marie went on smoking her cigarette.

Elopement plans

There was no legal reason why Carol should not marry Zizi; it was simply thought to be politically safer for the Crown Prince to find a foreign bride, preferably of royal blood. But in order to pre-empt his parents' certain veto, Carol decided to elope to Russia with Zizi and, as a cover, he enlisted the help of an army officer called Henri Serdici, who had a fiancée of his own in Odessa.

Serdici agreed to help by inviting Carol and Zizi to act as witnesses at his own wedding and obtained false passports for the party. Carol and Zizi evolved an elaborate plan in order to allay the suspicions of her mother. This involved her pretending to borrow his car on the pretext that she needed it to visit friends. In fact, she would collect Carol and Serdici, and the three of them would head for the border as fast as possible, hoping to reach it before anyone noticed.

A chapter of accidents

On the appointed day, almost everything went wrong. It was pouring with rain and the roads quickly became impassable. They had to borrow a horse and carriage and transfer to a train and, although they made it safely over the frontier at Bender, a suspicious German officer on the Russian side recognized the Romanian Prince. Carol decided on a bluff, saying that he was travelling incognito to the wedding of his friend. Fortunately, the officer – who, like Carol, had trained at Potsdam – respected the Prince's rank and took him to the regional headquarters.

Here they were warmly welcomed by General Zeidler, who insisted, however, on arranging their hotel accommodation in Odessa and detailed one of his men to accompany them. The man was obviously a spy but, under cover of his own wedding, Serdici managed to persuade

Popperfoto

👑 *Over six feet tall, blue-eyed and blonde-haired, Carol had grown into a dashing young man, far left, photographed with his mother Queen Marie in the grounds of the royal estate at Castle Peles. By this time, his family were already considering a suitable bride*

👑 *The Russian and Romanian royal families met in June 1914, above, hoping to arrange a match between Carol (standing fourth from left) and the Tsar's daughter Crown Princess Olga (seated third from left). But they were not attracted and it was not to be*

Popperfoto

QUEEN MARIE

Marie, Queen of Romania from 1914 until 1928, was a dominant force in Carol's youth and her warmth and intelligence, together with a formidable energy, made her extremely popular with the people. Granddaughter of Queen Victoria, before her marriage she enjoyed a glittering social life and her good looks attracted a string of admirers, including the American millionaire, Waldorf Astor. Ferdinand was no match for her wit or vitality and many people thought that she ran Romania, not he.

As Crown Princess and later 'the most beautiful Queen in Europe', she continued to win hearts. Among her most faithful male confidants was Baron Barbo Stirbey, brother-in-law of Carol's arch-enemy, Prime Minister Ion Bratianu. He trained Marie to look more closely at Romanian affairs and inspired her with his own fierce patriotism. One of Marie's greatest successes occurred at the Paris Peace Conference in 1919 when she used her persuasive diplomacy to gain large chunks of territory from Russia, Hungary and Bulgaria. After Carol's accession, he kept her from power, and she died after a long illness.

Popperfoto

Poppofoto

Poppofoto

👑 *In defiance of his parents'
wishes, Carol entered into a
romance with Zizi Lambrino,
above, sister of a childhood friend.
Although in theory there was
nothing to stop their union, it was
not thought proper for a royal
Prince to marry a commoner of
Romanian birth. To forestall
attempts to prevent the marriage,
Carol and Zizi eloped to Russia but
the escapade resulted in a court-
martial for Carol (then a serving
officer) and he was forced to agree
to an annulment*

👑 *After the annulment was finally
granted, the tall and handsome
young Prince was on his own
again,* left – *but not for long*

an Orthodox priest to marry Carol and Zizi in
secret without arousing any more suspicion and
the wedding day was set for 31 August 1918.

Just married!

Zizi made her own white dress from a few yards
of locally-bought *crêpe de chine* and she walked
to the Pokrowska Church wearing a raincoat to
hide it. Carol had her white shoes and stockings
in his pockets, and she changed into them in the
church before the ceremony, decorating her hair
with the traditional bridal orange blossom

Feeling very sick as a result of having eaten
bad crayfish the night before, she fainted twice
during the service. But she was determined that
nothing should spoil the day and, in the end, the
service was completed successfully, with great
charm. But as she was ruefully to recall later, the
happiness of marriage lasted just over a week.

The marriage is annulled

Carol sent a telegram to his father which read, 'I
am married to Zizi Lambrino. Reply if I may
return with her or if I must continue my journey
to France.' Carol knew that if he went back to
Romania he would face a possible court-martial
for deserting his post. He also feared that his parents would try to separate him from Zizi, but his
desire to stand by her was tempered by the fear
of losing his right to the crown.

When news of his wedding reached
Bucharest, his parents were deeply shocked. His
father showed him some sympathy, but Marie
accused Zizi of being nothing but an adventuress.
Parliament in Bucharest was equally opposed to
Carol's choice of bride and, in the end, Ferdinand
had to give way. Carol was sentenced to 75 days
in prison for desertion and proceedings were
started to annul his marriage.

'I am married...reply if I may return with her'

Carol and Zizi were enticed on to a train on
the Romanian border with a promise of a fair
discussion of their case. In fact, they were
trapped and Carol argued uselessly against a
decision that had already been made. After
several days, during which the train travelled
pointlessly from place to place, Carol was
escorted to a remote jail in the mountains while
Zizi had been sent home immediately she
crossed the border.

After this, although still legally married, long
bouts of separation from his wife, parental
pressure and uncertainty about his real aims
finally wore Carol down. He eventually agreed to
an annulment, although was not actually to take
place until after Zizi had given birth to his son,
Carol Mircea, on 8 January 1920.

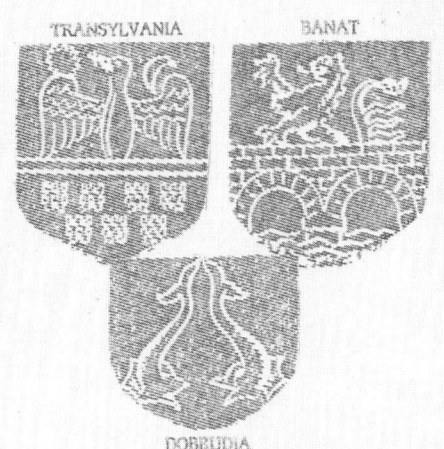

MOLDAVIA

TRANSYLVANIA   BANAT

WALLACHIA

DOBRUDJA

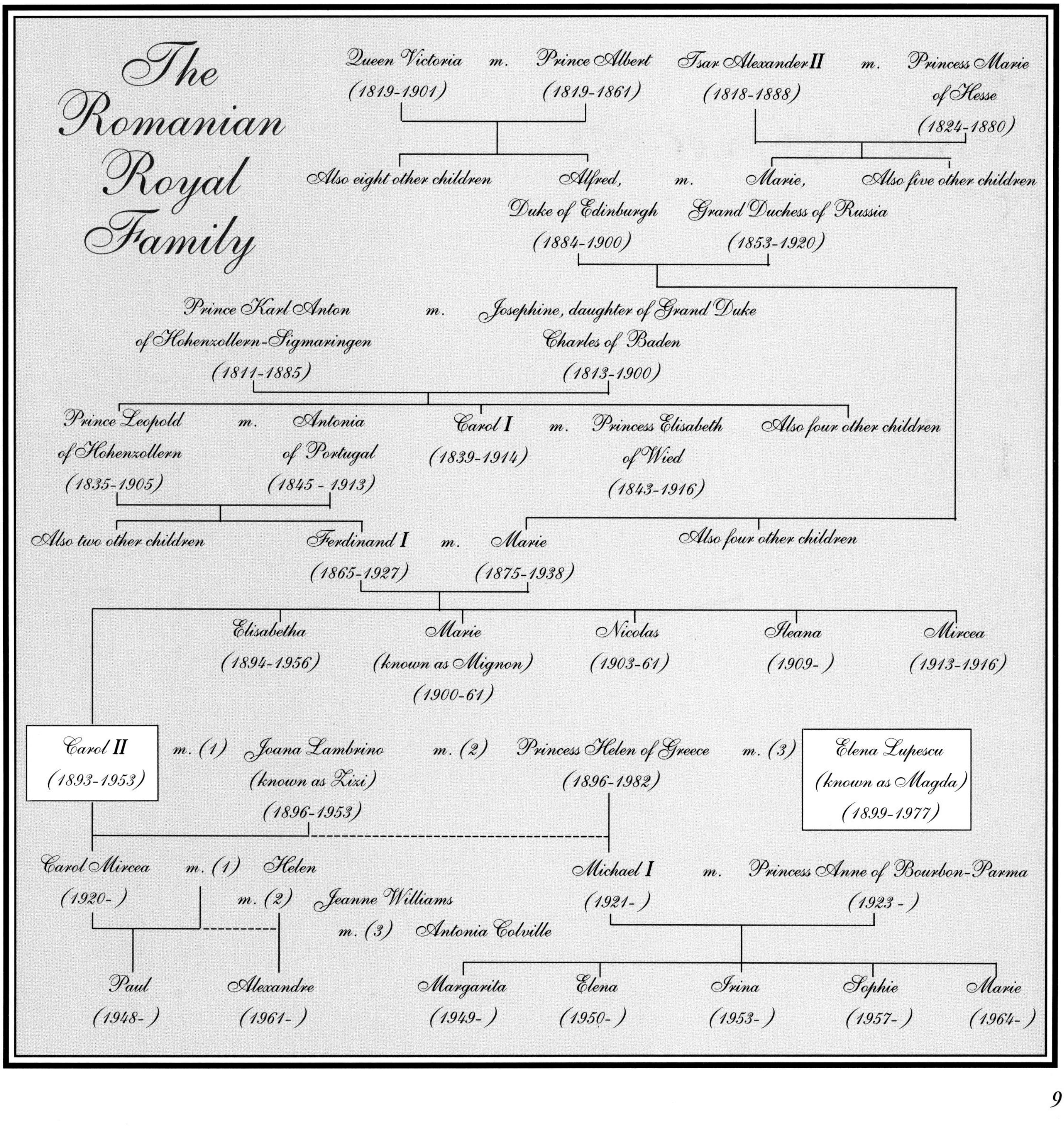

👑 *Romania was formed in 1862 by the coalition of the ancient provinces of Moldavia and Wallachia, right, that had formed part of the Turkish empire. In 1866, the country's royal dynasty was founded by giving it a German king of the Hohenzollern dynasty. Later treaties added the provinces of Dobrudja, Transylvania and Banat to the territory ruled by the Romanian royal family*

The Romanian Royal Family

Queen Victoria (1819-1901) — m. — Prince Albert (1819-1861)

Tsar Alexander II (1818-1888) — m. — Princess Marie of Hesse (1824-1880)

Also eight other children

Alfred, Duke of Edinburgh (1884-1900) — m. — Marie, Grand Duchess of Russia (1853-1920) — Also five other children

Prince Karl Anton of Hohenzollern-Sigmaringen (1811-1885) — m. — Josephine, daughter of Grand Duke Charles of Baden (1813-1900)

Prince Leopold of Hohenzollern (1835-1905) — m. — Antonia of Portugal (1845-1913)

Carol I (1839-1914) — m. — Princess Elisabeth of Wied (1843-1916) — Also four other children

Also two other children

Ferdinand I (1865-1927) — m. — Marie (1875-1938) — Also four other children

Elisabetha (1894-1956)

Marie (known as Mignon) (1900-61)

Nicolas (1903-61)

Ileana (1909-)

Mircea (1913-1916)

Carol II (1893-1953) — m. (1) — Joana Lambrino (known as Zizi) (1896-1953) — m. (2) — Princess Helen of Greece (1896-1982) — m. (3) — Elena Lupescu (known as Magda) (1899-1977)

Carol Mircea (1920-) — m. (1) — Helen — m. (2) — Jeanne Williams — m. (3) — Antonia Colville

Michael I (1921-) — m. — Princess Anne of Bourbon-Parma (1923-)

Paul (1948-)

Alexandre (1961-)

Margarita (1949-)

Elena (1950-)

Irina (1953-)

Sophie (1957-)

Marie (1964-)

Popperfoto

Popperfoto

Popperfoto

Popperfoto

👑 **Carol I**, above right, *first of the royal dynasty, was Carol II's great-uncle. His wife, Princess Elisabeth of Wied, appears at his side*

👑 *Carol's mother, Queen Marie, right, was Queen Victoria's grand-daughter and renowned as 'the most beautiful queen in Europe'*

👑 **The Romanian royal family was part of the Hohenzollern dynasty and thus had close links with the German royal line. In this picture Ferdinand and Marie are standing on the steps, surrounded by their children. Carol is second from right next to his uncle, Prince Karl-Anton of Hohenzollern. In the centre is the Crown Prince of Germany**

👑 *Carol had five brothers and sisters. Prince Nicolas, pictured, right, dressed in the uniform of a Roman soldier, completed his education in the British Royal Navy. His youngest brother Mircea, above right, tragically died at the age of three. Far right, Prince Carol and his sister Princess Elisabeth appear in the uniform of the Royal Hussars*

Family Album

In 1931, most of King Carol's family appeared at a gathering at Castle Peles in Sinaia, to mark the occasion of the wedding of Carol's youngest sister, Ileana, to Archduke Anton of Austria. In the front row, Carol's son Prince Michael stands next to his aunt Elisabeth and his father. In the centre, Ileana is flanked by the Archduchess of Austria, Queen Marie and the Archduke. Her new husband is standing behind, in the centre of a group of Ileana's sisters and their husbands

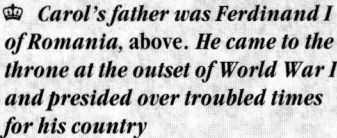

Carol's father was Ferdinand I of Romania, above. He came to the throne at the outset of World War I and presided over troubled times for his country

King Carol's second wife, right, was Princess Helen of Greece. His son by this marriage became King Michael I of Romania until deposed in 1947

Süddeutscher Verlag Bilderdienst

Popperfoto

Popperfoto

Magda Lupescu

Zizi was the first of two women who were to shape – and, some said, to destroy – Carol's life. The object of his second love affair was Elena Lupescu, known to the world as Magda. She was a real *femme fatale*, one of Europe's last great courtesans, and much more of an adventuress than Zizi had ever been.

Magda used to give various different dates for her birth, though the most likely were probably 1896 or 1899. Her birthplace was Hertza, a small Moldavian town where her father ran a chemist's shop. He was Jewish and his real name was Wolff, but he changed it to the Latin form of Lupescu to get a licence to trade in the region which, at the time, was severely anti-semitic. Lupescu converted to the Orthodox faith and married an Austrian Roman Catholic. Magda was the elder of their two children, the other one being a boy called Constantin.

Magda was still a child when her parents moved to the port of Sulina on the Black Sea. Part of the Romanian fleet was based there, and people said that half the naval officers who flocked to Lupescu's shop actually came to see his wife – not to buy his drugs. The story went that they would come in pairs and while Magda's mother 'entertained' one of them inside, the other would sit outside playing cards with her father.

A convent education

When she was 11, Magda was sent to a Roman Catholic convent in Bucharest, run by German nuns. She stayed there until she was 17 and learned to speak excellent German and fluent French. By 1912, her father had moved his business to Falticen and then Jassy, where he sold novelties and scents from a small shop.

The same year, Magda's mother took her to the mountain resort of Sinaia, where her striking looks and flirtatiousness won her immediate attention. She strolled about the town with three girlfriends, causing male hearts to flutter and eyebrows to rise; young unmarried women were supposed to be accompanied by chaperones.

Sex appeal

Magda gave small-town gossipmongers even more scope when she arrived in Jassy, which became Romania's capital after German troops invaded Bucharest. Though not conventionally beautiful, she had enormous sex appeal: a combination of flaming red hair, pale skin, light green eyes, and a voluptuous figure.

She also had a bawdy sense of humour, which made her a great favourite with the soldiers, though her detractors said she had a

Popperfoto

rasping voice and a violent temper, and was inclined to fat. She was certainly short, and this probably emphasized her weight, but her petite, Oriental figure would have been fashionable in an area of Eastern Europe that had once been part of the Ottoman Empire.

In the evenings, Magda would join the crowds of young people who paraded up and down Jassy's main street, or lean out of a first-floor window calling out 'Hi, handsome' to any good-looking man who strolled by. None of her flirtations was serious until she met an army officer called Tampeanu, who rapidly became obsessed with her.

Offers of marriage

Tall, thin and rather dull, Tampeanu pursued Magda doggedly with offers of marriage, until she accepted him in 1916. Poor Tampeanu

♛ *One of the last of the great courtesans, Magda Lupescu's early years gave plenty of scope to the gossip-mongers. Though not a conventional beauty, above, her flame-red hair, porcelain complexion and green eyes caused many a male heart to flutter*

♛ *Married to a Romanian army officer posted in Bucharest, the changing of the guard, far right, was to become an all-too familiar sight to Magda, who didn't hesitate to seek her pleasures elsewhere*

became the butt of many jokes, for Magda had no intention of changing her ways. 'It would take a *tampiteanu* to marry her,' said his fellow officers, making a play on the word *tampit*, which is the Romanian for an idiot.

Magda's marriage to Tampeanu lasted just four years, during which time he was relocated with his regiment to Bucharest. He had become very poor and quite unable to keep Magda in the luxurious style she wanted, while she, for her part, had been continually unfaithful to him. Their relationship ended in divorce in 1920.

Life in Bucharest

Known as the 'little Paris of the East', Bucharest suited Magda down to the ground. She made friends in its relaxed café society and idled away long hours flirting on the pavements of the Calea Victoriei, the capital's smartest street. She took up with new boyfriends and dropped them again with surprising ease. No one seemed to satisfy her for long. Not, that is, until she met Carol.

Illustrated London News

BUCHAREST: 'LITTLE PARIS OF THE EAST'

Hulton-Deutsch Collection

With its open-air restaurants and brasseries, wide boulevards, tree-lined streets and parks, Bucharest has often been described as the 'Paris of Eastern Europe'. Its most noticeable Parisian feature is the Triumphal Arch which was built on the Sosueaua Kiseleff in 1922 to celebrate the Allied victory in the First World War. It was designed by sculptor Petru Antonescu to imitate the Arc de Triomphe but the original construction in wood and stucco fell down and in the 1930s it was rebuilt in stone.

Though Bucharest could not rival Paris' chic it made up for this shortfall by sheer frenzy. Diners of the 1920s would be regaled by gypsy violinists or singers howling mournful folk songs at tops of their voices, while waiters and chefs screamed at one another and frequently came to blows. Young men would tear up and down the wide roads in racing cars, accelerating noisily past the sedate horse-drawn carriages, called *trasuras*, that were used by tourists for sight-seeing trips. At around 6 pm each evening, the smart set would promenade along the city's main shopping street, the Calea Victoriei. Sometimes the pavements became so packed that people had to fight to avoid the unthinkable fate of being pushed into the road among the less class-conscious.

THE CALL OF DUTY

**AFTER A SHORT, UNHAPPY MARRIAGE TO ZIZI LAMBRINO, CAROL
WENT ON A WORLD TOUR AND MET HIS SECOND WIFE, HELEN. BUT
THIS MARRIAGE WAS NOT TO PROVE A HAPPY ONE EITHER – AND IT
WAS THEN THAT HE MET MAGDA AND SWEPT HER INTO HIS LIFE**

Mansell Collection

Carol abandoned Zizi without even seeing his son. At his parents' suggestion,
he agreed to leave Romania for the best
part of a year and to travel round the
world. In theory, the purpose of this journey was
to establish trading links in the Far East, but for
Carol it was largely a sight-seeing trip. At first, he
wrote fervent letters to Zizi swearing his undying
love, but as his spirits rose these became less and
less frequent and finally stopped altogether.

He set sail from Constantza in February
1920, stopping off in Greece, Egypt and then
Eritrea before crossing the Indian Ocean for
Ceylon. From Ceylon, Carol travelled north into
India, where he was given a splendid welcome
and toured some of the country's famous shrines,
including the Taj Mahal.

The Maharajah of Patiala entertained him in
India at his luxurious palace and laid on a tiger
hunt, allowing him to watch the proceedings
from an elephant's back. Carol saw the
extraordinary ruined pagoda at Pagan in Burma
and in Malaya he met the fabulously wealthy
Sultan of Johore. Next on his itinerary were visits
to Hong Kong, Shanghai and Japan, and after this
he sailed to Hawaii and the USA.

Back in the more prosaic atmosphere of
London, he thought of Zizi again, sending her a
letter in which he expressed an uncharacteristic
note of caution. He advised 'courage and
patience', adding more affectionately, 'I adore
you (but) we must act with extreme prudence.'

Meeting with Helen

Then, three weeks later, on his way home to
Romania, he broke his journey to see his mother,
who was a guest of the exiled King Constantine
of Greece in Zurich. Carol's sister, Elisabetha,
had just become engaged to the King's eldest
son, Prince George, and Marie had gone to
Switzerland to discuss wedding arrangements.
Carol was struck by George's pretty younger sister, 24-year-old Helen, and within two months of

THE DISPOSSESSED HEIR?

The elder of Carol's two sons, Mircea, was brought up by his mother Zizi Lambrino. After her marriage was annulled, Zizi was forced to live in Paris to benefit from the financial settlement awarded to her until Mircea came of age. The legality of the annulment was disputed for many years, and much later two courts ruled that Mircea was, in fact, Carol's legitimate heir.

As a young man, he worked as a book-binder in Paris, but after his father's death, won the right to call himself a royal prince and changed his name to Carol Mircea. He bought a huge, secluded mansion in Dorset, England – where, in 1963, various English newspapers scurrilously linked his name to the Great Train robber Ronnie Biggs, who was apparently seen entering the grounds.

Carol Mircea married twice and had one son by each of his two wives, the elder of whom, Prince Paul of Hohenzollern-Romania, has written a biography of Carol II.

♛ *A world tour provided Carol with a welcome break from his tempestuous emotional life. Although officially, far left, he was a representative of Romanian interests, charged with setting up trade links, in practice he spent the best part of a year on what largely became a sight-seeing trip*

♛ *After stopping in Greece, Egypt and Ceylon, Carol received a splendid welcome in India. Here, he was entertained by the Maharajah of Patiala, who arranged for him to go tiger hunting from the relative safety of an elephant's back – a favourite pastime of royal visitors, above*

Popperfoto

his letter to Zizi, he proposed to her. Still in Zurich, he wrote to Zizi. 'It is not a conqueror who writes to you but a loser. . . Returning to the country, I saw that I had no chance of getting my way. I have therefore surrendered. The spell is broken. I have turned a new page. . .'

On her part, Helen's opinion of Carol was cool. She thought him 'retiring and not very affable.' But when Marie invited George and his sisters to her summer residence at Pelizor, near Sinaia, Carol insisted on travelling with them. Marie organized all kinds of excursions for the youngsters and noticed with satisfaction that Carol paid great attention to Helen.

Known to her intimates as 'Sitta', Helen was fine-boned, tall and slim, and very different in

> ## 'It is not a conqueror who writes to you but a loser... I have turned a new page'
>
> PRINCE CAROL TO HIS EX-WIFE ZIZI

character from Zizi. She had led a sheltered childhood, which had been cruelly interrupted by her father's exile. Now, she could relax at last among fun-loving young people of her own class. It was not long before Marie noted that her son and Sitta seemed to have come close to an understanding.

Family tragedy

But tragedy struck another blow when Helen's favourite brother, Alexander – who had remained in Greece as a figurehead King – was killed in Athens. He died of blood poisoning after trying to rescue his dog from a monkey that bit him as well. On hearing this dreadful news, Helen and her sister naturally wanted to go straight home to their family in Zurich, and Carol offered to accompany them. As he was boarding the train, Princess Ileana flung her arms round his neck and whispered that he should bring Sitta back with him. Carol, who was now a broad-shouldered and moustachioed 27-year-old, asked Helen to marry him and she accepted.

Carol's proposal came at a difficult time for Helen, for whom a royal prince was an eminently suitable match. Whether her love for him was real or not, he offered her at least a temporary shelter from the uncertainties in her life. At first, at any rate, the couple seemed genuinely passionate about each other. Carol would stride about like a despot, with an adoring Helen completely in his thrall, happy to take his lead in everything.

Popperfoto

♔ *Returning from his tour, Carol stopped to meet his mother who was arranging the betrothal of her daughter Elisabetha to Prince George of Greece, right, son of the exiled King Constantine. There he met George's pretty sister Helen, seen, above, in Macedonian peasant costume. Tall and fine-boned, she seemed to be a perfect match for Carol and within only two months, he proposed*

♔ *Helen, right, was prompt in her acceptance of Carol's proposal. It came at what was, for her, an uncertain and difficult time – offering a welcome respite*

Repercussions

In his final letter to Zizi, he wrote, 'It is true that I am engaged, and engaged to a princess. That is so against my principles that I am myself even the most astonished... I have found someone who can understand me and who in the theories of life has the same ideas as I. She has agreed to be the consolation of a heart profoundly bruised...'

Zizi's response was to agitate for a financial settlement, and her protestations were eventually rewarded when the King's advisors placed an annuity for her in a Paris bank. They allowed her enough income to help her support Mircea while he was growing up, but deducted the value of Queen Elisabeth's jewels, which Carol had given her and which she refused to return. (These were said to be the last gems of the royal family left outside Moscow.) Zizi had no choice for the moment but to accept these terms and went to Paris, where she stayed for the rest of her life.

Helen's father had agreed to the marriage, provided that Carol had really got over his affair with Zizi. For their part, his parents were overjoyed: here, at last, was a perfect wife who would

> ## '*I fought a mighty battle for you, to put you back on the straight road*'
>
> CAROL'S MOTHER QUEEN MARIE

make an admirable future queen. They breathed a sigh of relief and Marie set to work on the practical business of arranging two weddings.

Double wedding

After Alexander's death, the Greeks had given their monarchy an overwhelming vote of confidence and King Constantine had been restored to the throne. So Helen and Carol celebrated their nuptials at the Metropolitan Cathedral in Athens – but, instead of the double ceremony which was laid down as law by the Orthodox Church for occasions when sisters and brothers of two families married each other, their wedding took place on 10 March 1921, two weeks after Elisabetha married Prince George. It was a glorious occasion and crowds lined the streets as they passed, but Greek peasants saw this break from tradition as a bad omen.

A week beforehand, Marie had written to Carol in the strongest terms she could muster, hoping to remind her errant son of his duty. 'I fought a mighty battle for you, to put you back on the straight road, Now it lies before you to walk straight upon it.' As time would prove, she might just as well have saved her energy.

Popperfoto

Carol and Helen honeymooned for a week at Tatoi, an estate owned by the Greek royal family just outside Athens, then went back to Bucharest. Meanwhile, a temporary home was prepared at the Foisor, a dingy Swiss chalet built by Carol I in the grounds of Castle Peles.

Seven months later, Helen gave birth there prematurely to Carol's second son on 25 October. They called him Michai, the Romanian form of Michael, after a national hero who had united the provinces of Moldavia, Transylvania and Wallachia in the 16th century.

Never very robust, Helen was exhausted after an excruciatingly painful labour and rested for several weeks. As she slowly recovered, a house was found for the young family in one of Bucharest's smartest quarters. Marie hired Harrods of London to carry out a complete renovation of their new home but Carol brought Helen and Michael there in December 1921, before the decorations were finished.

Helen was still unwell and could face neither her husband's enthusiastic love-making, nor the chaos in her household. She asked King Ferdinand for permission to visit her parents in Greece and went away for four months, taking Michael with her.

Carol's new love

Shunned by Helen, Carol sought amusement elsewhere and, by the time she returned to Romania, his name was already linked with that of another woman.

Some of his time was devoted to charity work and promoting Romanian culture, and it was through these occupations that he first met Magda, then Mrs Tampeanu, in 1923. The story goes that she engineered an invitation to one of his charity galas by using one of her current boyfriends to escort her there. The man was a photographer called Postmantir and he often took pictures for the Prince's charities. When he tried to get her a seat with a good view of the stage, she demurred, puzzling him by opting for a place far back and halfway behind a pillar.

As he discovered later, her aim was not to look at the performance at all, but to be seen herself. She was in Carol's direct line of vision, and gazed at him throughout the evening without once dropping her eyes. The Prince could not fail to notice her, and squirmed under her relentless stare, glancing at her covertly to see if he could recognize the flaming redhead who seemed so interested in him. But it was she who made the next move, with a similar performance at another charity gala.

She was not disappointed and, shortly afterwards, Carol persuaded a friend of his to throw a party and invite her along. This friend was Captain Tautu, a disreputable seadog who, it seemed, plied the Mediterranean for the sole

Popperfoto

♛ *On 10 March 1921, with King Constantine now restored to the Greek throne, Helen and Carol,* left, *were able to marry in Athens Metropolitan Cathedral. The occasion was glorious; the bride radiant. Little did she know how short-lived her marriage was to be*

♛ *Helen's son Michael,* above, *heir to the Romanian throne, was born on 25 October 1922 after a long and difficult labour. The strain on Helen was enormous and her relationship with Carol was never quite the same*

♛ *Despite their problems, Helen and Carol had shared happy moments together, as this picture,* left, *shows. But by the time she had recovered from the stress of childbirth, her husband had already found a new love*

CAROL THE PUBLIC BENEFACTOR

It would be quite wrong to give the impression that Carol was only interested in gratifying his own more frivolous desires. He was, in fact, an important figure at the head of Romanian public life and was personally responsible for setting up several sporting, cultural, military and educational institutions including a university and a church.

In 1913, Carol had founded the Romanian equivalent of the Boy Scout movement, a mere five years after Baden-Powell had set up the original in England. In 1918, he helped form the Sports Federation for young men aged between 18 and 30, and established a charitable organization with the aim of providing help for young students. Thanks to an interest in aviation, he was also instrumental in setting up the

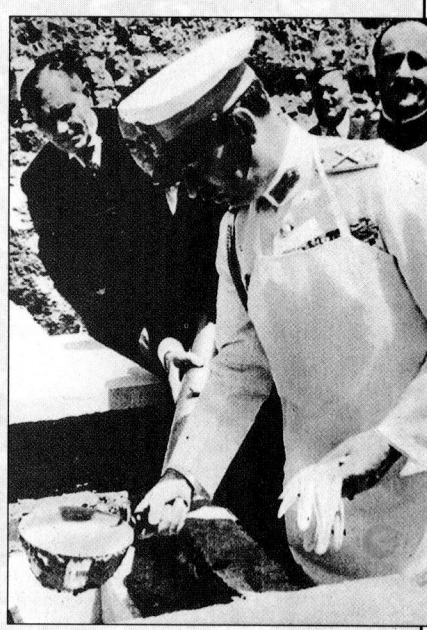

country's first military air corps and took a continuing hand in the development of the Romanian air force.

In 1921, the year of his marriage to Helen, Carol founded the Royal Cultural Foundation, which highlighted his interest in fostering Romanian culture, both at home and abroad. One of the principal aims of the foundation was to safeguard the traditions of village life in the countryside, while another was to promote the translation of foreign works of literature into Romanian. He also created a publishing house to provide educational books for the peasantry and in 1922, founded he Philharmonica Orchestra.

purpose of chasing women. He had been known to change his course to gratify his lusts and once dropped anchor in mid-course because a female passenger refused to give in to him. Legend has it that the other travellers, sick of waiting to reach their destinations, begged her to relent so the ship could proceed. Apparently she did.

Captain Tautu owned a flat in Bucharest, which was known intimately to most of bohemian Bucharest who often came to let their hair down amid its exotic decor and tiger skin rugs. Magda had been to the flat many times and Tautu certainly knew her well. It was said that the Captain had been one of her mother's lovers in Sulina, when she was a little girl and he had no illusions about Magda's reputation.

The captain's party

Magda arrived on the evening of the party wearing a demure white dress which showed off her hair and her milky skin to perfection – and hardly spoke a word. Letting Carol talk without interruption, she fixed him with her limpid, emerald green eyes. Completely taken in, Carol feasted his eyes on her ravishing face and figure, and thought her the wittiest girl he had ever met.

When the party drew to a close, he was deeply smitten and offered to drive her home. She hesitated for a moment and then said no. Coyly, she asked him what people would think if they were seen together. After all, Carol was a married man, as well as the Crown Prince.

Captain Tautu overheard this exchange and was horrified. He could see Magda's game but he had not bargained on its effect on Carol. The situation called for drastic action and he took it. Waving his arms wildly he swore at Magda, calling her a dirty whore. She is reported to have said, 'Who will protect the honour of an innocent woman?' but Carol gallantly came to her aid – sweeping her out and into his life for ever.

A stormy relationship

Carol's parents knew that his marriage was unstable, but they had no idea just how rocky it had become. After he met Magda, he hardly saw Helen and Michael and stopped sleeping with his wife altogether. To friends, he confided that she repelled him, saying that she gave him 'gooseflesh', whereas Magda's earthy vulgarity made him feel like a real man. Even so, he kept the affair secret for two years. Finally he could stand it no longer and confessed his loathing for Helen to his parents. It was then that the storm broke about his head for the second time.

♚ *Magda Lupescu, right, set out to captivate Prince Carol from the first, when she engineered an invitation to one of his charity galas and arranged a seat so that she was directly in his line of vision. Whenever the Prince looked up, there was Magda returning his glance, fixing him with her green eyes*

👑 Castle Peles stands on a small
hillock high up in the pine forest of the
Carpathians. Designed in 1873 for Carol I as a
summer palace, the building displays an amazing confection
of styles inside and out. Its roof is covered with turrets and pinnacles, while
the facade boasts Turkish and Renaissance originals and the furniture was
mostly Gothic revival. The windows are brightly stained glass and Queen
Elisabeth devised a colour scheme for the interior of old gold and moss green.

👑 Despite the rather
overbearing, oppressive
surroundings inside the
castle, there were homely
havens of tranquillity.
This is part, *right*, of the
personal salon of Queen
Marie, Carol's mother

👑 More typical of the
decor is the timbered
ceiling, heavily carved
overmantel and gallery
in the salon, *far right*,
occupied by Carol's wife
Helen as the Crown
Princess of Romania

CASTLE PELES AND VICTORIEI PALACE

During his years of exile, Carol lived in many parts of the world but his most important residences inside Romania were Castle Peles, where he was born and met Zizi Lambrino, and the Victoriei Palace in which he lived during his reign. Both are now museums

♛ The Victoriei Palace in Bucharest, *below*, is an impressive building with a rather austere, classical exterior in the classical style. Queen Marie, who found Romanian palaces oppressive, described it as 'squat, low and of no distinctive style'. Three-sided, it was built around a square with a fountain.

♛ The library, *bottom*, was decorated in the same heavy style as most of the interior of the Palace, with a deeply carved and moulded wooden ceiling and walls which were characterised as 'all windows, doors and fixtures'

♛ The monumental staircase, *below*, leading to the King's apartments, was one of the finest features of the Victoriei Palace and was untypically light and airy. Most of the decor tended towards black marble and dark, heavily carved timber

All pictures from the Illustrated London News

A COUPLE IN EXILE

**BY THE TIME CAROL'S AFFAIR WITH MAGDA LUPESCU BECAME
PUBLIC KNOWLEDGE, THEIR EXILE WAS A FOREGONE CONCLUSION.
IN PARIS, THE COUPLE ADOPTED AN INDOLENT, IF FRUGAL,
LIFESTYLE AND CAROL LAID SECRET PLANS FOR HIS RETURN**

Illustrated London News

👑 *Crown Prince Carol was one of the four kings and 11 heirs to the throne who attended Queen Alexandra's funeral when she was laid to rest in Westminster Abbey in 1925. He appears on the right in the second rank of the procession. This was to be Carol's last official engagement before a life in exile*

Ferdinand and Marie met Carol's announcement that his marriage had failed with heavy hearts. They had heard all this before when Carol was involved with Zizi Lambrino and in their eyes it was the second time their son had forsaken his royal duty. Though far from happy in her relationship, Helen was devastated, but she received scant sympathy from her parents-in-law who merely told her she was lucky: after all, unlike them, she had only been let down by Carol once.

Try as they might, neither his parents nor his wife could persuade Carol to give up Magda Lupescu. His fascination for her and her hold over him were based on two factors: she made him feel independent and she mothered him. There was no contradiction in this, for until Carol met her he had suffered from a sense of frustration that had its roots in his strained upbringing.

Magda's down-to-earth personality must have come as a breath of fresh air to Carol. Though he rebelled once, he obviously still saw himself as a dog who had been brought to heel and deeply resented the constrictions of his royal role. His father could still identify with him but even Ferdinand had to admit defeat over the Lupescu affair. He voiced the picturesque but damning verdict that Carol was as full of holes as a Swiss cheese. Queen Marie was ruder and her relations with Carol grew openly hostile as she tried using her political influence with Prime Minister Ion Bratianu, Stirbey's brother-in-law, to get rid of Magda. There were also rumours that Carol's mistress had been 'planted' on him deliberately by communist authorities in the Soviet Union. This and many other stories became part of the lurid mystique that enveloped Carol's love for his glamorous companion.

Escape from duty

It was two years before their affair became public and, in the autumn of 1925, Carol told his parents that his marriage was effectively over. The only solution seemed to be a temporary separation and when Edward VII's widow, Queen Alexandra, died in November that year, Carol went to London to represent his family at her funeral. Helen did not go with him, nor did Magda, but the trip gave Carol the escape route he was looking for. He was supposed to wait in England to accompany his younger sister, Princess Ileana, home from boarding school at the end of the winter term. Instead, he telephoned the school on the day he was due to collect her with a message that he had made alternative plans for her journey and would not be coming after all. He then crossed the Channel for Paris and a different rendezvous.

Nobody knows if Carol really planned his next escapade in advance. Perhaps events gathered momentum as he went along, gradually getting out of control, so that his exile was a foregone conclusion before he had time to think about its possible consequences. What happened was this: Magda travelled to France by rail with one of Carol's cars that had been loaded on to the train. He picked her up in Paris and they then drove to Italy together. On arrival in Milan, they booked into two separate rooms in the same hotel. Legend has it that Magda gave her name as Princess Lupescu and, though this is unlikely, the couple were frequently seen in Carol's car and made little effort to hide themselves away. But it was definitely in Italy that Elena Lupescu earned her nickname of Magda, when an Italian reporter confused her with a Polish circus performer who had visited Milan shortly beforehand.

A public scandal

News of Carol's 'scandalous' affair had already been splashed over English papers; now it broke for the first time in Romania's press. At first, journalists in Bucharest told the nation that its Crown

♛ *The Crown Prince became Mr Carol Caraiman – now simply a Romanian private citizen living abroad,* above. *His first move was to Paris, which in the late 1920s was an exciting and bustling city – an easy place in which to get lost,* below

Illustrated London News

Prince had fled to Milan with Zizi Lambrino. This was a reasonable error to have made since his ex-wife was known to be living in Paris. But when they learned her true identity, few people had a kind word for Magda Lupescu.

The Romanian Prime Minister persuaded King Ferdinand to order Carol home at once, without his mistress. But though a high-ranking general and a close friend both went to Milan to talk him round, Carol remained adamant. He would not leave Magda; he would not even discuss it. The second of the two negotiators could not get past Carol's door, which was kept resolutely shut. The Prince repled to his written entreaties with a note that read defiantly: 'You will have to bring me home in my coffin.' Emotional, heart-felt letters came from Helen and slightly more manipulating ones from Queen Marie, but Carol ignored all their appeals.

His own answer to the problem was dramatic and totally impractical. He offered to pretend to be killed in a boating accident and disappear without trace. His parents dismissed this idea without a second thought, but Carol's determination to stay with Magda played into his enemies' hands. If he would not let go of her, they said, he would have to renounce his right to the throne.

Permanent exile

In the end, he not only lost his royal claim, but membership of the royal family as well. On 4 January 1926, Crown Prince Carol of Romania became plain Mr Carol Caraiman, a private citizen travelling abroad, condemned to permanent exile. His four-year-old son Michael was proclaimed heir apparent and a Regency Council was appointed to act for him in the event of Ferdinand's death.

In one of her rare interviews with the press at the time, Magda said she had had nothing to do with Carol's renunciation. But it was clear that without her, he would never have taken such a fateful step. And no sooner had the necessary documents been signed than he began to regret his impetuous decision and to hope that it could be reversed.

Whatever Carol's future held in store, he now had to face the day-to-day reality of his new status. Living in expensive hotels had eaten away most of his funds and his first step was to take Magda back to Paris, where he could draw on a legacy that had been left to him by his great-uncle, Carol I. With this steady, if reduced income, the young couple started to look in earnest for a house.

Setting up home

They eventually chose a ten-room, partly furnished villa on the Boulevard Briot in the north-western suburb of Neuilly. The house was soon filled with a grand piano, tapestries, oil

The exiled Prince and Magda enjoyed a close companionship but remained figures of public interest despite Carol's removal from Romanian politics. Here they were photographed, above, ***in the South of France for the popular weekly paper,*** The Illustrated London News

Walks in the Bois de Boulogne, illustrated, right, ***in a contemporary French magazine, became part of the couple's indolent Parisian lifestyle***

Mary Evans Picture Library

Hulton-Deutsch Collection

👑 *Carol had always delighted in anything to do with driving, and had taken part in races at Cluj in Romania. Here he indulges his interest in cars at the Automobile Salon in Paris, trying out the Constantinesce gearless car with guidance from its inventor*

paintings, ornaments and books. Even though they were now technically part of the bourgeoisie, they wanted to maintain a regal appearance and the result, not only at Neuilly but also in all their future homes, was rather heavy, dark and cluttered.

In Paris, they settled down to an indolent and surprisingly frugal lifestyle. Carol would rise at noon and, after a leisurely breakfast, they would take their dogs for a walk in the nearby Bois de Boulogne. In the afternoons, they would ride horses, play tennis or go for a drive before returning home for dinner with a few guests, then play bridge late into the night. They both liked the cinema, while Carol was fond of classical music and reading about military history. He was also free to devote himself to another great hobby – stamp collecting, which he enjoyed for many years to come. Magda's literary preferences ran to sensational novels, particularly the those of the French novelist, Dekobra.

Simple tastes

Magda also prided herself on being an efficient housekeeper (her passport described her as 'housewife') and she enjoyed preparing typical Romanian dishes for their meals. But she kept quarrelling with their servants and a steady stream of cooks, housemaids and butlers came to the Boulevard Briot only to leave days or even hours later. It was the same at the Château de Coesmes, the mansion in Normandy that Carol had purchased as a country retreat shortly after moving to Paris. In one of his rare notes of pessimism about her, Carol mentioned Magda's

Illustrated London News

Popperfoto

👑 *Despite her disapproval over Carol's conduct and his affair with Magda, Queen Marie was soon reconciled with her eldest son and appeared in public with him, above, on the eve of her departure for America in October 1926. Prince Carol is standing on his mother's right, wearing a bowler*

👑 *When Zizi Lambrino, herself now living in Paris, left, heard that Carol was in France, she instigated an unsuccessful legal action against him in an attempt to gain revenge for his desertion*

unfortunate temperament in a letter to his mother. But she was still the lynch-pin of his life, and in any case, the absence of domestic staff meant they could make a useful saving in wages.

For all his reputation as a playboy, Carol had fairly unsophisticated tastes. He preferred beer to champagne, disliked nightclubs and hardly ever gambled. True, the couple were often photographed at fashionable French resorts but for everyday life, Magda dressed down without flashiness, minimizing her bills for ordinary clothes. On the other hand, Carol expressed his love for Magda by giving her expensive jewels – and in public she wore silks and furs bought from top designers. Magda always wore very high-heeled shoes but this was not so much a fashion statement as a way of increasing her height as, in normal heels, she was dwarfed by Carol who towered above her, over six feet tall.

Political ambition

Their circle of friends came from the Parisian nightclubbing set and the sizeable community of exiles who had fled from authoritarian regimes in their own countries. While he enjoyed their company, Carol also kept in touch with Romania, where many people had refused to accept his renunciation. Those closest to him wrote to him loyally as if he were still the Crown Prince and, with their help, he started to test the air in case he could return to Bucharest.

Magda encouraged his ambition and tried to impress Romanians who longed for a 'macho' leader by spreading exaggerated tales of her lover's satyr-like sexuality. But at home with Carol in France, she took charge of him and kept a close watch on all his political contacts. She even went as far as monitoring his conversations from a hiding place behind some bookshelves. If a 'dangerous' subject came up, she would interrupt loudly, astonishing the unsuspecting visitor and perhaps embarrassing Carol as well.

Fate takes a hand

When his ex-wife Zizi Lambrino heard that Carol was in France, she tried to avenge herself for his desertion by starting a legal action against him. This was unsuccessful, but Carol was still married to Helen and, incredible as it seems, she wrote him fond, encouraging letters, begging him to come back to his country if not to her. In fact, they had already agreed to divorce. Both his father and mother visited him secretly in Paris, and he convinced them that it was useless to try to persuade him to take Helen back. He did not divulge his other intentions. Then early in the morning of 20 July 1927, King Ferdinand died. He had been ill for some time but the news hit Carol twice over and, while genuinely grieving for his father, he felt the full bitterness of his decision to give up his rightful inheritance.

♛ *Magda made the most of a short stay in England, where she enjoyed the peaceful country life in South Godstone, Surrey, above. She enjoyed the company of her hostess, Madame Ionescu, below (far left), and her family, pictured on a visit to London Zoo*

But events began slowly to go his way. Just four months later, Carol's rival Prime Minister Bratianu died when a throat infection turned into blood poisoning. With Bratianu out of the way and his father no longer on the throne, the prince felt able to gamble on his popularity in Romania. However, he waited until the next spring before taking definite action.

Exiles in England

On 28 April, he boarded the SS Jan Breydel in Ostend and sailed to Dover. He obtained a two-month visa, saying that he was there to visit friends. Magda travelled with him, as well as her father, younger brother and six servants. The party also included wealthy businessman Barbu Ionescu and his wife, who had a mansion at South Godstone in Surrey. Ionescu had made most of his money from the catering trade but he had a dubious reputation, which ran from broth-el-keeper to imposter. It was also suggested that he was the illegitimate son of a former Romanian Prime Minister. Nevertheless, Carol was short of influential helpers and needed him.

Carol and Magda were supposed to stay with the Ionescus for a week. On the Monday after his arrival, the ex-Crown Prince and his mistress were spotted at the Strand Theatre in London, watching a performance of *The Monster* starring Ruby Miller. Under the heading 'Madame Lupescu in Royal Box', *The Daily Sketch* reported that she wore an ermine coat trimmed with fox and quoted the admiring comments of several bystanders who were not only struck by her 'beauty and her wonderful golden hair' but also by her 'charm and simplicity.'

Planning a coup

Speaking to reporters, Carol said that he had come to England because his mother was English and because he loved the country. He also said all he wanted was a quiet life with absolutely no involvement in politics. But this was just a smokescreen. Though the couple danced at the Savoy and took tea with friends, Carol was busy with plans for a dramatic coup. He had 20,000 copies of a manifesto printed, setting out a programme of reforms for Romania and stating that Magda had definitely not caused his exile in 1925. 'I want to do my duty to my people and my country. I want to return with your consent.'

One of Carol's friends chartered two commercial aircraft from Imperial Airways, to be ready at Croydon Airport at dawn on 6 May. Carol planned to board one of the planes and fly to Romania. The other was to carry his proclamation leaflets and scatter them over the town of Alba Julia, where a National Peasant Party congress was due to commence the same day. (The Party's members represented Carol's closest political allies in Romania at this time.)

♛ **Carol takes a walk in London, top,** *with his temporary host Barbu Ionescu, a wealthy businessman with a dubious reputation.*

♛ **In 1927, Prime Minister Bratianu,** above – *leader of the Liberal Party and Carol's rival – died, leaving the way open for him*

♛ **At home with the Ionescus, right,** *Carol laid his plans in secret*

Hulton-Deutsch Collection

But his plan backfired. The British Foreign Office got wind of his secret and prevented him even reaching Croydon. Undercover agents had been tracking his movements ever since he arrived in England and the whole operation had a marvellous whiff of cloak-and-dagger mystery about it. The Foreign Office used the lame excuse that Carol had not obtained an entry visa for Romania. In fact it was more likely that they did not want Britain to be seen to be abetting an event that might upset the Romanian government. Someone managed to smuggle a few copies of Carol's manifesto as far as Switzerland, but by that time they would have been too late for the congress. His attempted coup failed.

👑 *Croydon airport, above, was the scene of a daring escapade which was to have seen Carol flying back home in triumph, but the plot was foiled by undercover agents of the British Foreign Office*

👑 *The exiled Prince had planned to appeal to a rally of the National Peasant Party at Alba Julia, right*

Illustrated London News

Carol deported

On 16 May, Carol was officially deported from Britain for his 'unfriendly' political activities. He and Magda were escorted on to a cross-Channel ferry by two detectives but, instead of going back to France, he decided to make for the Château d'Ardennes near Namur in Belgium, the home of another rich supporter. His failure was a major setback, and his mother wrote to tell him that she was ashamed of his behaviour 'in her own country'. She did not add that she had apologised for him personally to King George V, but he replied with equal vehemence that it was

Illustrated London News (colour retouching by Bill Payne)

THE PEASANT UPRISING

At the turn of the century, Romanian politics were dominated by two political parties: the Liberals, representing powerful, industrial and urban influences; and the Conservatives, party of the landowners and gentry. Neither stood for the interests of the largely peasant population and, in 1907, this resulted in a bloody uprising – bordering on civil war – which was violently put down by the Liberals with the acquiescence of the Conservatives. One result was the growth of the National Peasant Party. This had the support of the rural working classes and grew out of the merger of several minority parties. In 1917, they were swept to power.

Unlike many constitutional monarchs, Carol was free to follow any political persuasion he chose, and from the early 1920s demonstrated that his sympathies tended towards the National Peasant Party led by Juliu Maniu. However, taking such a position was certainly not wise and did not help Carol's cause after the Liberals returned to power in 1922. Although Ferdinand's views tended towards those of his son, he wisely kept silent, while Marie had long shown her Liberal preferences.

Illustrated London News

only a matter of time before everyone agreed with him. In fact, he had to bear two more years of frustration before realizing his ambition. Later that summer, Carol and Helen were divorced.

Now that Bratianu was dead, Romanian leaders were divided and the country seemed on the verge of collapse. King Michael was only seven years old and the Regency was ineffective. So Maniu, who led the National Peasant Party, offered to let Carol return if he would make three promises: to let his son keep the crown; to try to repair his marriage to Helen; and to abandon the evil Magda Lupescu. By the summer of 1930, Carol was so desperate for an active role in Romania that he gave in to all these requests.

Parted from Magda

Meanwhile, the Romanian government tried to bribe his mistress into leaving Carol. It was said that Constantin Dimitresco, a Romanian student who had wormed his way into Carol's confidence, used his friendship with the American dancer, Loie Fuller, to find a patron willing to finance a new life for Magda in British Columbia.

An American millionairess apparently volunteered for this service but Magda was not to be bought and, in early June 1930, she saw Carol get into his car and drive away from his château in Normandy. He was on his way to Munich, a halfway stop before a short flight to an air force station near Cluj in his homeland. It had been a

long, anxious five-year wait and perhaps Magda wondered if she would ever see her lover again.

Carol landed in Romania in the late evening. He changed into uniform and was met just outside Bucharest by his younger brother, Prince Nicolas. They drove together straight to the Cotroceni palace and as soon as people heard of his return, a wildly enthusiastic crowd gathered. Carol was still popular and as his mother, the former Queen Marie, had already left to visit friends in Bavaria, there was no one to object to his presence in the royal quarters.

It was soon clear that Carol had no intention of keeping all his promises to Maniu. On 8 June, he deposed his son, giving Michael the imposing but largely meaningless title of Grand Voevod (Prince) of Alba Julia. He met Helen only once, and though he tried to persuade her that a reconciliation with him would be good for Michael and Romania, she refused: she had spent too long fighting for a divorce to change her mind.

The question of Magda Lupescu hung in the air like a lowering cloud. Finally it was too much for Carol, who burst out in front of his ministers that he could not live without her: 'She is the other half of my being, the other half of my mind'. The Prime Minister did the only thing he could now Carol had let him down: he resigned, and the country was plunged into turmoil. But far from the man who was causing such an uproar on her behalf, Magda had disappeared.

Popperfoto

👑 *Following the death of King Ferdinand, the Council of Regents had appointed Carol's son Michael, top (far left), as King. But Michael was still a child and this arrangement was ineffective to deal with the country's problems.*

👑 *After he had agreed to many concessions, Carol was allowed to return and was warmly greeted by younger brother Nicolas, above*

GRAND STYLE

In the years between the World Wars, many European monarchs still aspired to the extravagant manner of an earlier age, and Carol loved to dress in uniform to suit the occasion. But Magda, the commoner who became his consort, reflected the changing values and style of a modern age

Plumed cavalry helmet

Honours, medals and orders of merit

Sash is not only decorative but also serves the function of holding up the sword

♛ Carol wearing the uniform of a Romanian Field Marshal from 1938. His passion for uniforms even extended to designing them himself, and when living in an apartment in London, he had a dressing room specially adapted to house his vast collection

Cloche hat was one of Magda's favourite styles

♛ Magda's station meant that she never had to appeared officially with Carol, leaving her free to dress in the carefree manner which she favoured. This Paris day-dress is of a style which she enjoyed during her years in exile there, for it flattered her short figure and emphasized her striking colouring

Green and pink set off Magda's unusual colouring

Drooping skirt and sleeves compose a very feminine figure

Flower-patterned silks were popular at this time

High-heeled court shoes give added height

♛ In later years, Magda dressed simply, befitting her status as the mistress of an ex-King in the years of post-war austerity. Even so, she managed to maintain a certain style. When pictured in this travelling suit on board ship in October 1947, she and Carol had with them an amazing 65 suitcases, 35 trunks and 45 huge crates of luggage

Popperfoto

Illustrations by Mario Teppema Strang

GATHERING STORMS

CAROL RETURNED TO ROMANIA, WHERE HE TOOK ON THE ENORMOUS TASK OF TRYING TO PUT THE COUNTRY BACK ON ITS FEET. THREATENED BY THE IMPENDING WAR IN EUROPE, THE KING TURNED TO MAGDA FOR COMFORT AS NEVER BEFORE

Illustrated London News

👑 *On 8 June 1930, Carol attended a special session of Parliament and took the oath as King of Romania,* above. *With brother Prince Nicolas at his side, he toured the capital in the royal coach, dressed in the uniform of a General of the Airforce,* right

Illustrated London News

Almost as soon as Carol had dashed away from Normandy, Magda was besieged by reporters who wanted to know where he had gone and what was to happen to her. Instead of facing them, she kept her front door closed and said nothing. Days later, she travelled mysteriously to Interlaken in Switzerland, where pursuing journalists lost her trail. In fact, she was making her own arrangements to obtain a visa and follow Carol across the Romanian border. She only re-emerged some weeks later when he was already in Bucharest.

Magda was political dynamite and Carol was well aware of it. During his ten-year reign, he always set great store by appearances and, from the start, he tried to keep her a secret. Once again, she retreated into the background of his life as she had done when they first met. She did not accompany him openly to public functions but palace servants knew that she could often be found sitting behind a curtain on a private balcony to listen to the proceedings from a safe distance. She lived in a house on her own, only seeing Carol after dark when she was fetched to the Palace by chauffeur-driven car. She would return to her own home near Modrogan park later that night, or in the early morning.

Gloomy splendour

Carol, meanwhile, occupied a comfortable villa called the Casa Nona in the grounds behind the main Cotroceni Palace complex. The palace itself was unattractive, with a low, squat-pillared facade on the outside fronting a set of depressingly sparse state apartments, which the new King used only for official business. The interior walls of these rooms were hung with religious paintings acquired in a job lot by Carol I who just wanted pictures to cover the many large bare spaces. There were several El Grecos among this mottley collection, but at the time the old King bought them, he was a forgotten artist, and apparently no one realized how valuable they were until Carol II removed them in 1940.

Carol's son Michael lived in the villa as well and a tug-of-war began between the boy's parents when Helen, deprived of the child she had nurtured alone, demanded to see him more often than Carol wished. Carol hoped that Michael would grow to like Magda but, with Helen around, this was impossible. She hated her and tried to make sure that her son felt the same way.

The banished wife

In the summer of 1931, after Helen had flouted his strict regulations several times, Carol's patience ran out. He banished her from Romania altogether, sending her first by train to a siding in Sinaia where she was given four weeks to make her plans. Helen eventually decided to settle in Italy and Michael was allowed to visit her for a month twice every year. Even so, she returned to Romania to see him there several times.

While this new family drama was unfolding, Carol had decided that Michael would have a truly democratic education. He ordered that special classes be arranged for his son at the palace with a group of children who were drawn at random from widely differing social backgrounds, including peasant villages.

In trying to put Romania back on its feet, Carol faced a task of Herculean proportions but his reforms, though idealistic, were impractical. He had been aware of the poverty in the country's rural areas for a long time and organized a scheme that he hoped would solve the problem.

Illustrated London News

Süddeutscher Verlag Bilderdienst

♔ *King Carol always enjoyed ceremonial occasions and had a large collection of uniforms. At a cavalry review, above, he appeared in the uniform of the Romanian Horse Guards and the cloak of the Order of Michael the Brave – a Romanian folk-hero after whom Carol had named his son. On the left, he appears in the uniform of the* Chasseurs de Montagne

Hulton-Deutsch Collection

Illustrated London News

♚ As King, Carol did much to promote national culture and pride. Top, *he tours a cookery contest in Bucharest with the wife of Prime Minister Tatarescu.* Above, *schoolchildren parade in formation to spell out the King's monogram at a national festival.* On the right, *the King receives a petition from a peasant leader*

♚ *Meanwhile, powerful and disturbing factions were providing an alternative to Carol's policies, notably the Iron Guard, led by the fanatic Codreanu,* opposite top

He sent young people to the villages to teach the inhabitants how to cook more nutritiously. But the instructors used sophisticated utensils and food not normally available to the peasants, who looked on with understandable scepticism, so the exercise was largely useless.

Carol also paid great attention to one of his pet interests, the armed forces, and spent a lot of time and effort each year re-designing the uniforms of various regiments. Though he began his reign with great seriousness, the government of Romania gradually broke down into groups of small, oppposing factions that were ripe for exploitation by the power-hungry nations who crowded its borders.

Magda's unpopularity

When Carol's mother returned from her vacation in Germany, she accepted the new sitution with typical clear-sightedness and some trepidation. One of Carol's first acts in taking over the palace had been to rip out her private telephone link to Baron Stirbey and in 1931, his right-hand man, Dimitresco, tried unsuccessfully to kill Stirbey while he was travelling west on the Orient Express. Carol's attitude to Marie and her friends gradually hardened. He forbade her from taking part in politics or public life and set up a spying system to report on her and to intercept her letters. Marie was not alone in believing Magda was responsible for his antagonism.

As Carol's reign developed, Magda was blamed for everything that went wrong in Romania, but few people dared to criticise him or his mistress openly. Using the excuse that he needed greater authority to pull the country together, Carol became increasingly tyrannical, controlling the army and the secret police. And behind all the grandiose pomp and ceremony of the many state occasions at which he asserted his authority, he was accused of corruption.

Of course, the stories may well have been exaggerated to make them them sound more impressive but it is certainly true that, aided by Dimitresco's manipulative hands, Carol encouraged a sycophantic following of hangers-on. From her impotent position as Queen Mother, Marie scathingly called his entourage a collection of 'pimps and parvenus' and certainly this description matched stories that the revenue from Bucharest's brothels went straight into Carol's pocket. He was also accused of siphoning off vast amounts of money from businesses and sending it abroad, either to secret foreign bank accounts or the safe-keeping of friends.

A wily manipulator

While she indulged herself at Carol's expense, Magda was not without her own trials in Bucharest, most of them originating from the wily Dimitresco. But in 1932, having been continually rude about her behind her back, he made the dangerous mistake of insulting her to her face, whereupon Carol dismissed him at once, much to Magda's satisfaction.

Dimitresco was soon replaced by a man called Ernesto Urdareanu who, to the many cynical observers outside the King's charmed circle, seemed even more grasping. He was a cavalry officer who snatched at the chance to profit by Dimitresco's fall and, by ingratiating himself with the king, rose to a position of power in the palace guard. He became Carol's general factotum and it was common knowledge that anyone who wanted favours from the King would first have to court, and possibly, bribe Urdareanu.

Strange attractions

Carol and Magda's relationship was puzzling. On one hand, they gave the impression of being inseparable and their union outlasted many conventional marriages. On the other, Magda treated him with contempt and her violent outbursts often reduced Carol to quivering jelly. There was a famous and often-quoted occasion when Prince Michael was roused from his sleep at Casa Nona one night by the sound of sharp cries and thundering footsteps. When he looked round his door, he was amazed his father careering naked down the passage with Magda in hot pursuit waving a gun.

With Urdareanu acting as a buffer between him and the country at large, it is no wonder that Carol grew remote from his people, but while his erratic methods of government have been severely criticised, no one could accuse his reign of being dull. While he was on the throne, 18 prime ministers came and went from office, and

Hulton-Deutsch Collection

LUPESCU'S WILD PARTIES

Hulton-Deutsch Collection

While living as Carol's mistress in Bucharest, Magda was not allowed to appear with him in public. But she was not the retiring kind, and became notorious for holding rowdy, all-night parties at her house on the Avenue Vulpache. Her 'court' included bohemians and sycophants who wanted to curry favour with the the King, and tongues wagged as strains of wild, gypsy music floated out on the respectable air of Modrogan Park, the smart district where she lived.

The world's press gave Magda the cruel title of 'she-wolf', a play on both her father's surname Wolff and her wicked reputation. When she left Bucharest in a hurry, her house stood empty in its large walled garden and snoopers came to inspect her lair. They were disappointed to find the place dark and badly furnished (one said it resembled a second-hand furniture store) – though her bedroom, with its beautiful grey silk bedspread, was more elegant. Magda had a direct telephone line to several of Carol's rooms at Cotroceni Palace as well as his villa.

Rex Features

♔ *Treading a political tightrope, King Carol attempted to maintain his neutrality in the face of threats from both Germany and Russia. Top, he visits the German leader and his Foreign Secretary von Ribbentrop at Berchtesgaden in November 1938.*

♔ *But in 1939, as the German storm troops invaded Poland, above, smashing all opposition, Carol realised the hopelessness of Romania's position*

one was assassinated. One of the most disturbing elements in Romanian politics during Carol's rule was the rise of the Iron Guard. This movement had been founded as a relatively harmless form of nationalism shortly after the First World War, but while Carol was King, it took on a truly terrifying character. Its spiritual leader – a young fanatic called Corneliu Codreanu – created a gang of right-wing toughs named the Legion of the Archangel Michael.

Powerful enemies

During the early 1930s, the Legion was integrated with the Iron Guard and became the Romanian equivalent of the German Nazi party or Italian fascists. Codreanu was handsome and exuded romantic charisma. In order to win the support of the peasants, he would gallop into rural villages on a white horse, dressed entirely in white and holding a religious icon aloft. Codreanu convinced many simple people that he was the incarnation of the Archangel Michael without saying a word; his dazzling appearance and burning eyes were enough.

While Carol dismayed his subjects with his roller-coaster tactics and authoritarianism, the Iron Guard seemed to present the only united, stable alternative. By 1937, it was widely represented in Parliament with over 60 members and,

strangely, even Carol gave the impression that he approved of its policies. But he knew that the Guard was financed almost completely by the Nazis, that they thought he was weak, and that they had vowed to destroy Lupescu as well as all the Romanian Jews. So he played a double game.

As Hitler grew more aggressive, Carol tried to steer a neutral path between him and Stalin in the Soviet Union. Between them, these two threatened Romania's hard-won provinces – not to speak of its rich oil fields. At the same time, Carol also turned to Britain and France for aid.

He seemed to have appeased Hitler as well, but then Carol flung Codreanu and his closest henchmen into jail, promising to ensure their safety in return for German support in the event of a European war. But two days later the imprisoned Guardists were killed in suspicious circumstances and it was assumed that they had been murdered on the King's orders.

The net closes in

From then a net began to close in and Carol turned to Magda for comfort as never before. He wrote in his diary at the start of 1940: 'Our love has stood like a rock... and has been for me the essence of life, a divine talisman and a supreme refuge in the most difficult times. This love is such that I cannot conceive of life without it.'

Suuddeutscher Verlag Bilderdienst

Associated Press

Popperfoto

Hulton-Deutsch Collection

Hitler invaded Poland and although Britain and France declared war on Germany, they were not prepared to bolster Romania. The country was helpless and Carol felt he could only wait and hope. Fearing attempts on his life, he gave up hunting – a favourite pastime – and began to hoard provisions. Hitler declared Transylvania part of Hungary and the Soviet Union demanded the return of Bessarabia plus part of Bukovina, denuding Romania of more than half its lands.

In a desperate bid to placate Hitler, Carol appointed the pro-German, viciously anti-semitic Ion Antonescu as Prime Minister. But Antonescu proved the last straw in the King's line of defence and instead of supporting him as he promised, he tried to divest Carol of his executive powers. When Carol refused, the Prime Minister requested his abdication. Twenty-four hours later, on 6 September 1940, Carol capitulated. The next day he published a proclamation announcing that he had stepped down from the throne in favour of the 18-year-old Michael.

A desperate escape

Suspecting that the Prime Minister would conduct a witch-hunt for Magda and perhaps have him murdered as well, Carol arranged for their immediate departure by train to Yugoslavia. He recalled Michael's mother Helen and Magda tried to reassure Michael that he would be able to manage on his own, saying he only needed courage and all would be well, while this was probably his father's last chance to escape alive.

Stokers kept the engine at full steam as the royal party filled nine carriages with their belongings. Apart from Carol, Magda and the faithful Urdareanu, the party included four military aides, some servants and five dogs. Their luggage comprised everything of value that they could carry: pictures by El Greco, the royal jewels and, some said, a fortune in foreign currency.

Finally, they slid away from the station, but Carol's nerves were still on edge. When the train pulled into Lugoj, he was told that the Iron Guards had planned to board it to kidnap Magda, and that they would try again at Timisoara, the last big town before the Yugoslavian frontier. Carol posted nine guards with machine guns at the train windows and ordered the driver not to stop until they were well into Yugoslav territory.

As they drew into the station at Timisoara, the train slowed down and Carol heard shots, which he identified as the type of German guns normally used by the Guardists. The driver put on speed and Carol's soldiers fired back through his compartment's barricaded windows. He lay on the floor and Magda crouched low in a metal bath while their attackers pursued them right into Yugoslavia where, luckily, soldiers on the border fought them off.

Safe at last

The royal train halted safely and the men who had protected Carol so loyally on the journey were advised not to return to Romania, where they would almost certainly have been under sentence of death. Meanwhile, Prince Paul, Yugoslavia's Regent, sent a general to escort Carol and Magda safely to Italy. Their troubles were over – temporarily at least.

👑 *King Carol and Prince Michael put a brave face on the mounting crisis, reviewing troops wearing the new steel helmets that he had recently introduced,* top left. *But the reality of Romania's position was revealed,* above, *by the pitifully inadequate border defences, known as Carol's Dyke.*

👑 *Politically outmanouevred and with the country on the brink of disaster, Carol was forced to abdicate. With his beloved Magda at his side, he began a desperate escape attempt using a specially chartered train,* top

♛ As a respected collector, *above*, Carol was elected a member of Britain's respected Royal Philatelic Society in May 1948 and two years later, in May 1950, became a fellow of the Society while he was in London for the Grosvenor House exhibition. His fellowship was proposed by Sir Geoffrey Duveen and seconded by Sir John Wilson, the Keeper of the Queen's stamps – then President of the Society

♛ In addition to his own interest Carol himself was also the subject of a rich variety of Romanian stamps, now treasured by collectors. This set of four stamps, *right*, dates from 1937 and commemorates the 17th birthday of Crown Prince Michael. The overprinted values represent a postal price increase. Interestingly, the portrait at top left is taken from the official photograph used on Carol's passport

♛ Many special stamps were issued to mark the tenth anniversary of Carol's reign, on 8 June 1940. Ironically, this occasion occurred a scant three months before Carol was forced into exile in favour of his son Michael. The stamps themselves commemorate happier times and show Carol as a powerful leader and benefactor of his people. The examples shown here include such activities as his foundation of the Scout movement, and his efforts on behalf of the church, medicine and the armed forces

Ray Duns

A KING'S COLLECTION

Throughout his life, Carol was a passionate stamp collector. When he first went into exile, his mother Queen Marie initially objected to him taking the collection out of the country but later relented. During Carol's years away from Romania, it remained a point of contact between them and she often sent him new examples. In later years, Carol was forced to sell part of his treasured collection to raise money and sadly, after his death, the remainder was dispersed for ever

♔ At the Grosvenor House exhibition in 1950, Carol displayed a frame of Moldavian stamps and covers in the Court of Honour, reserved for the best exhibits. His entry attracted special mention in the *Index to the Best Known Stamps and Rarities in the Exhibition*, particularly for the unique *tête bêche* pair of the 27p stamp

Topham Picture Source

♔ This set of eight stamps, *left*, is for different denominations of *leu* (or *lei*) the Romanian unit of currency. Note that there are two values printed on each stamp. This is because the postal system was also used as a means of raising charitable donations – which went to different beneficiaries, depending on which issue of stamps was purchased. In this case, the money raised was provided for the aviation fund

Ray Duns

Thanks to EURO-YU Stamp Collecting, 138 New Bond Street, London W1 for supplying the stamps on these pages

JOURNEY'S END

**IN EXILE FOR THE SECOND TIME, CAROL AND MAGDA SETTLED IN
RELATIVE COMFORT IN MEXICO, WHERE THEY WERE MARRIED AT
LAST. BUT THE STRAIN OF THEIR UNCERTAIN EXISTENCE WAS
BEGINNING TO TAKE ITS TOLL ON THEM BOTH**

♛ *After fleeing across half of
Europe, ex-King Carol and Magda
Lupescu crossed the Atlantic
abouard the SS Excambion from
Lisbon. Magda is seen here,* above,
*with some of the many friends that
the couple made on the voyage*

♛ *Carol takes part in the lifeboat
drill,* above right, *with fellow
passengers on the Excambion.
After the rigours of their escape,
the risks of the voyage must have
seemed small by comparison*

Carol's first aim was to get as far away
from Hitler as possible. Crossing the
north-east corner of Italy, he, Magda
and Urdareanu went to Lugano in
Switzerland and then on to the south of France,
which was then in the power of the Vichy government (and therefore controlled by the Nazis).
On 12 September 1940, they made their way into
Spain, reaching Barcelona two days later.

Spain had taken a neutral stand between
Germany and the Allies, but it was ruled by the
dictator General Franco, who had been support-
ed by Hitler and Mussolini during the Spanish
Civil War. However, Carol was reasonably confi-
dent that Franco and his Foreign Minister would
be sympathetic and, indeed, this proved to be
the case, even though, once there, he was not
allowed to leave. Back in Romania, Antonescu
accused Carol of absconding with state funds and
demanded his extradition from Spain so that he
could be brought to trial. This did not happen,

partly because, having just rid himself of Carol,
Antonescu did not really want him to return – but
it made the exiled King feel extremely vulnerable
at what was, for him, a difficult time.

Moving restlessly from place to place, Carol
settled temporarily with his small entourage in
the ancient city of Seville. But even in Spain's
deep and remote south, he felt uneasy. He realized that the Germans, through their friendship
with Franco, were probably keeping a close eye
on him. Although he was free to travel around
Spain, a policeman was assigned to follow him –
ostensibly for Carol's protection but the man was
detailed to act as an informer as well. To add to
Carol's frustration, he had been ordered to tell
the authorities about his movements in advance.

He decided to solve this irritating problem
by going further west to Portugal as soon as he
could. His first step was to write complaining of
his plight to the Papal Nuncio in Madrid and
Prince Paul of Yugoslavia, and to ask them to use

Popperfoto

♚ *Arriving in Havana, Cuba, during May 1941, Carol and Magda spent some time in relative comfort. But their relaxed air, above, did little to conceal the fact, uppermost in their minds, that they were still on the run*

their influence on his behalf. Meanwhile, Urdareanu was sent to Lisbon to seek permission for the exiled King's entry into the country with his mistress and to arrange visas for them.

On the run

Everything seemed to be ready as Carol prepared for another dramatic escape in late February 1941, but a devastating hurricane blocked the mountain passes out of Spain and forced him to postpone his departure for a few more days. Urdareanu had stayed in Portugal all this time to smooth the way for his arrival with Magda. At half-past three in the morning on 3 March, Carol told his apparently imperturbable bodyguard that he was driving to a town called Lerena, which is about halfway between Seville and the frontier at Badajoz.

The man did not object, and in fact no one made any attempt to stop Carol's escape throughout his journey, though it can hardly have been a secret. Their route and a provisional

timetable had been prepared for them by a Colonel Jurawscki, thought to be a member of the Polish Secret Service. He had written this on a small piece of paper and Carol noticed Magda clutching the scrap nervously in her hand as they streaked westwards through the early-morning sunshine. They had stuffed the car with their belongings, trying to make them as inconspicuous as possible, and Magda was sitting in the back to act as lookout. Jurawscki had allowed them just two and a half hours to drive into Portugal before the frontier posts were fully manned.

In fact, Carol made it to the first scheduled stop with time to spare, handling his vehicle expertly as he followed the tortuous bends over the Sierra Morena to meet Joly, their companion on the next leg of the journey. While Joly drove them as far as the outskirts of Badajoz, his chauffeur took care of Carol's car, leaving it and their luggage to be collected later at a petrol station in the border town. For this part of the trip, the former King of Romania lay down on the back seat, covered by a rug, and Magda sat beside Joly.

Crossing the border

When they reached their second rendezvous at 5.20 am, there was no sign of the man they expected to meet, Rente, an invaluable guide thanks to his experience as a smuggler and friendship with the border police. Several tense minutes passed before they found him nearby.

Rente was the proud owner of a battered old banger, which had a hidden compartment underneath the back seat. It was in this cramped box, lying flat out and bumping uncomfortably a few inches above the pitted road, that Carol and Magda made their undignified trip across the border. Some way before reaching the Spanish customs, Rente had stopped to pick up a Portuguese guard who wanted a lift back into his own country. This man acted as an unwitting guarantee of safe passage and the car swept through the checkpoints unhindered.

A few miles further on, Rente dropped off the guard and opened the back seat. His secret passengers were able to breathe freely again and said a fervent prayer, thanking God for their salvation. At the town of Elvas, they met Urdareanu, and Tente drove all three to his farm, where they waited once more for Joly who was to take them into Lisbon. Rente's final task was to pick up Carol's car from the petrol station in Badajoz.

Farewell to Europe

Carol told the Portuguese authorities about his entry on 5 March, but in fact he stayed in the country for just under two months. Even though he was on the very edge of Europe, the continent still seemed dangerous to the ex-King and the government in Lisbon irked him by restricting his involvement in politics.

Topham Picture Source

The trials of war

Fighting on the German side had caused horrendous casualties in Romania and, by 1945, Michael was able to rally enough backing from a few opposition members to have Antonescu arrested. It was an incredibly brave act and for a while it paid off, even though German planes bombed Bucharest in revenge. Michael formed a coalition government and, declaring his support for the Allies in a radio broadcast, mobilized the army to reclaim Romania's territory from the invaders. His success did not last long, however, for Stalin's Communist Party quickly began an insidious infiltration of the whole government system and though Michael resisted as best he could, the Soviet stranglehold proved far stronger than him. After a two-year war of nerves, he was forced to abdicate and, in January 1948, he went into exile.

The scarlet woman

Carol's efforts on Michael's behalf had met with polite rebuffs. No heads of state were rude enough to say so to his face but the reason was of course, his betrayal of his country and his wife for Magda. Even though they now lived together as respectably as any staid married couple, Carol's lack of morals had profoundly shocked a large section of American society. Many people in Europe, too, still regarded him as totally unreliable. Inevitably, comparisons were made between him and Edward VIII, who renounced the British crown in 1937 to marry a divorced woman, Wallis Simpson. Magda and Wallis were seen as the two most 'scarlet' women of their era and, whether or not they merited it, newspapermen the world over fed off it hungrily. Scurrilous verse about Magda appeared in the English press and Carol was credited with the dictum, 'When in Rome do as the Romanians do.'

Magda's illness

Magda had shown many times that, in spite of her much-publicized feminity, she was both tough and resourceful. Although she lost a lot of weight and looked stunning in public, however, the strain of her uncertain existence began to make her ill. The Mexican climate did not suit her either and Carol was worried enough to suggest a change. He too was unhappy and frustrated by his inability to make anyone listen to his ideas, but this was 1944 and he could not yet risk a return to Europe. Barred from his first choice, the USA, Carol made for the Copacabana Palace hotel in Rio, accompanied by Magda, Urdareanu and his new young wife, Monique, and a staggering 115 trunks and suitcases.

Brazil's tropical summer heat affected Magda as badly as Mexico had done. Carol thought about moving to Argentina but its climate would have been no better. Magda became

So, packing their bags again, the couple went to Cuba at the start of May, relaxing for a few days in the American Virgin Islands and Bermuda on the way. But their journey actually continued until August, when they reached Mexico and made a longer halt. They still had Urdareanu in tow to organize the practicalities of their lives and, with his help, they found a house in the smart Coyoacan district of Mexico City, which they rented for the next three years.

Living in relative comfort among friendly people, Carol and Magda enjoyed themselves by going to race meetings and throwing parties. Urdareanu acted as their Lord Chamberlain, helping to maintain the illusion that their household was an outpost of the Romanian royal palace. Though he had abandoned Michael to a very uncertain fate, Carol now used his position as ex-King to try and help his son.

From exile, he wrote to heads of government in Europe and the USA, as well as other European monarchs, to enlist their aid. He also planned an organisation called the National Council of Free Romania, with the aim of restoring Michael to his rightful position. He received occasional letters from his son and Helen but meanwhile Michael had taken his own initiative.

♛ *After spending three years in Mexico City, Magda was suffering from the climate and Carol suggested a move to Rio de Janeiro in Brazil. Here they enjoy a trip aboard a motor-boat, above, a brief moment of relaxation shortly before Magda became seriously ill with pernicious anaemia.*

♛ *Frightened by his beloved Magda's close encounter with death, Carol asked her to marry him. A quiet civil wedding in their hotel bedroom in Rio during 1947 was legitimised in the eyes of God by the head of the Romanian church in Paris in 1949, far right*

♛ *Marital union suited the couple, right, even though their close companionship withstood many trials and tribulations for 22 years before the knot was tied*

weak and depressed, but none of the doctors she consulted could find the cause of her sickness. During her life, Magda had made many enemies but now, as she was rumoured to be dying, her numerous friends showed their affection in letters and telegrams from all over the world. A message from Barbara Hutton, the Woolworth heiress, read: 'Sweet and lovely friend, am so distressed at your illness and want you to know that all my heart, thoughts and prayers are with you.'

Effecting a cure

In early 1947, by which time she was spending most of each day in bed, Magda's mysterious ailment was finally revealed: she had pernicious anaemia. While Carol was advised that there was no cure, Magda found a Hungarian doctor in Rio who gave her blood transfusions and thus saved her life. At the same time, frightened that he might be losing his beloved for good, Carol proffered his own original form of treatment by asking her to marry him.

After 22 years of close companionship, this gave Magda a wonderful psychological boost and went a long way towards restoring her happiness. A quiet wedding took place in their hotel

Süddeutscher Verlag Bilderdienst

Süddeutscher Verlag Bilderdienst

on 5 July 1947; and from then Magda became known as Her Royal Highness Princess Elena of Romania. Taking the doctor's advice that his wife would continue to suffer if she stayed in the tropics, Carol decided to head for Europe.

The war was now over and he applied to France and Portugal for permission to enter both countries. As the Portuguese replied first, he accepted their invitation and he and Magda made their home together at the villa Mar Y Sol in Estoril, together with Urdareanu and his wife. Here, too, the former king of Romania moved in the familiar society of other exiled royalty. His

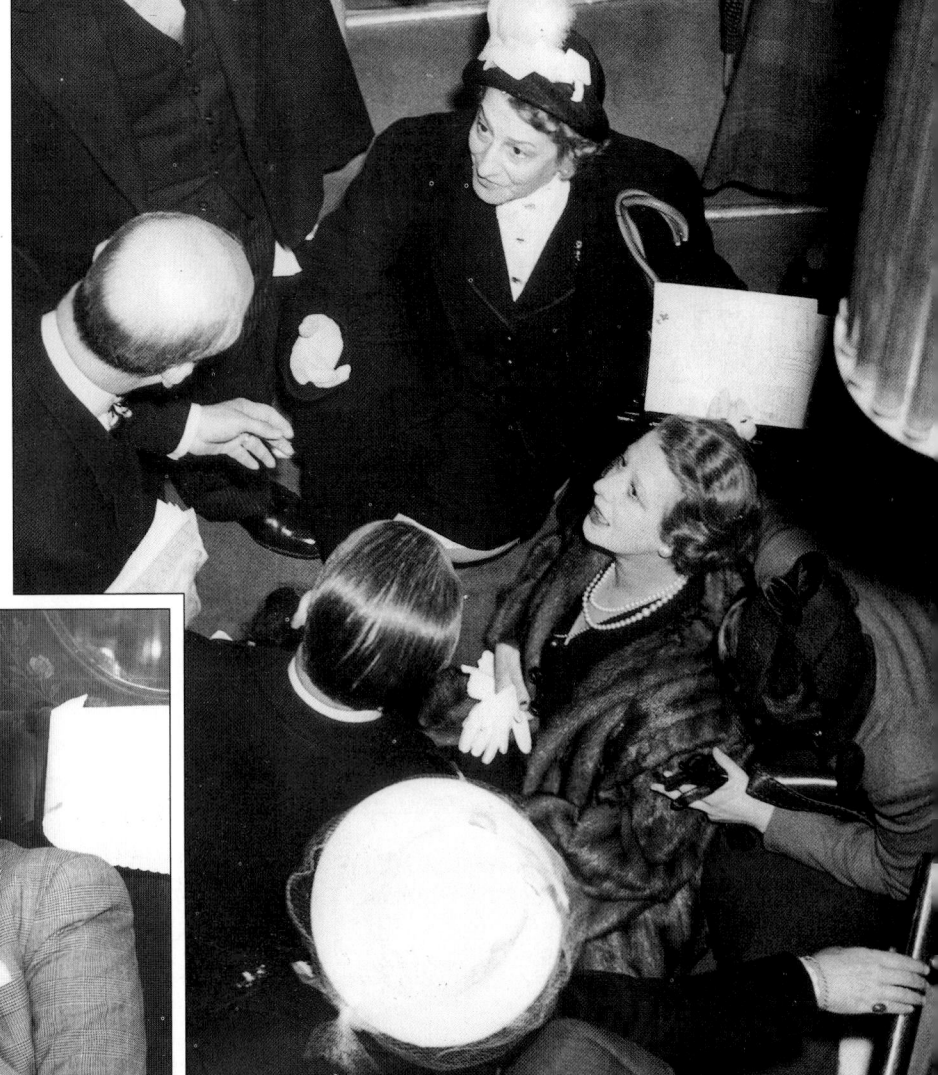

Topham Picture Source

Popperfoto

♛ *On 5 May 1950, ex-King Carol of Romania and Magda, who, as his wife, was now known as Princess Elena, arrived in London for the International Stamp Exhibition at Grosvenor House,* above. *The ex-King, himself a keen philatelist, lent a number of valuable stamps to the exhibition*

♛ *While attending the exhibition, Magda caused concern when she slipped and fell on the stairs, breaking her ankle,* above right. *In fact she recovered quite quickly, but by this time, Carol himself was becoming seriously ill*

♛ *Carol died on Good Friday 1953, in Lisbon. He was 59. In a poignant ceremony on 7 April, Magda sprinkled Romanian soil on her late husband's coffin,* right, top. *Other mourners at the crowded funeral,* right, bottom, *included Carol's brother Nicholas (left) and nephew (right), the son of his younger sister Marie*

CAROL'S VANISHED FORTUNE

Ever since he fled from Bucharest in 1940, Romanians have speculated on the fate of Carol's wealth. Prime Minister Antonescu accused him of absconding with state funds, and it was said that after milking the nation for his own benefit and sending the proceeds abroad, he stripped the Palace of every portable asset, including a vast amount of foreign currency and paintings by El Greco, similar to the well-known example seen here. And when he fled to Lisbon he was supposed to have left behind huge amounts of cash.

But Carol was continually short of money while in exile. In the late 1940s, he criticised Magda for overspending and was refused access to a bank account in the USA. To raise cash, he had to sell several houses left him by his family, as well as his precious stamp collection. It is possible that any hidden riches were whittled away by those to whom he had entrusted them for safe-keeping.

El Greco: The Burial of Count Orgaz. Toledo, S. Tome/Bridgeman Art Library

friends included Umberto, the deposed King of Italy, the Count of Barcelona, and the Comte de Paris. Magda and Carol became fanatical cinema goers, sometimes watching the same film several times, and the local cinema proprietor reserved special seats for them.

Otherwise their lives seemed to be gradually moving apart; Carol had given up any idea of going back to Romania and concentrated on his garden and his stamps. It was said that Magda had become a stickler for protocol to underline her grand status and that she spent vast amounts of money. Rumours started up about them once more: Magda never stopped nagging Carol, she embarrassed him in public, he berated her for overspending, they were going to divorce.

Blessed by the Church

Instead, Carol confounded all the gossip by arranging to marry his wife again. The ceremony in Brazil had only been a civil one. Now he would confirm his love for her in the eyes of God. He asked the head of the Romanian church in Paris, Father Martinian Ivanovitch, to conduct the service at their villa in August 1949. On the day of the ceremony, Magda looked radiant and far younger than her 53 years. She wore a satin dress with a lace bodice and her hair was set off by a fine veil of Alençon lace. Carol put on a morning suit and white tie but although obviously content with the woman who had stood by his side for so long, his face was haggard.

In 1950, he and Magda visited a stamp exhibition in London. Though Magda caused a minor sensation when she fell down some stairs and broke her ankle, Carol seemed withdrawn. In fact, he was showing the early signs of a fatal illness but, like Magda several years earlier, no one could find anything wrong with him.

Death of the king

In March 1953, he complained of chest pains, but when he consulted a Lisbon clinic, his tests were negative. Three weeks later, on Good Friday, Carol felt a severe pain in his left side and arm. A doctor was called in but, once more, his examination revealed nothing amiss. Carol said: 'Don't worry about me. Look after the Princess who has had a bad shock.' The doctor turned away. Moments later, Carol died without making a sound, after a massive heart attack. It was nothing more than coincidence that exactly a week earlier, his first wife Zizi Lambrino had also died poverty stricken in a Paris hospital, but many people saw a kind of poetic justice in Carol's death so soon afterwards.

Magda bade Carol farewell adding 'love of my life', as she watched his coffin being lowered into its sarcophagus. She was dressed in sombre black from head to foot with a veil over her face which had no make-up, and she was sobbing

Popperfoto

Topham Picture Source

Camera Press

⚜ *After her husband's death, Magda stayed on alone in their villa in Portugal. She outlived her beloved Carol by 24 years*

uncontrollably. After a crowded funeral, Carol was buried in the Royal Panteon at the Sao Vicente Monastery, alongside the Kings of Portugal to whose dynasty he was related by marriage. Nobody who knew the recent history of the Romanian royal family was surprised that his son Michael did not attend the service.

Childless and with only the Urdureanus as close companions, Magda stayed on at her villa in Estoril, confusing biographers and curious journalists by weaving improbable stories about her origins and upbringing. She once 'confessed' to being the illegitimate daughter of King Carol I and a village teacher; then she claimed to have been sent to Bucharest's most exclusive convent school. These lies were all part of the grand image she herself wanted to believe in and, by the end of her life, they were harmless enough.

People often wondered whether she had returned Carol's love or whether she really was as black as the ruthless, self-seeking adventuress that the press had painted. And while his attention may have lapsed from time to time, Carol's devotion to this remarkable, tenacious and colourful woman cannot be in doubt. Magda Lupescu fell asleep for the last time on 28 June 1977. She was 81 – as far as anyone knows.

KING MICHAEL'S RETURN

After years of obscurity behind the Iron Curtain, Romania made the international headlines again when Ceausescu was deposed in 1989 and a new, more liberal regime was installed. One belated beneficiary of this may be Carol's son King Michael, who possessed the distinction of being the sole surviving head of state from World War II and the last monarch of an Iron Curtain country.

After his brave stand against the Nazis and the communists, Michael abdicated in 1947. He went to live in England, where he tried farming. Other occupations included being a test pilot, running an electronics firm and working as a stock broker.

One of the slogans of the anti-Communist revolution was 'We want bread and Michael,' but ironically his return was not initially welcomed by the new regime, who had him deported following an unscheduled visit to Bucharest on Christmas Day 1990. In January 1991, news broke that the 70-year old King, a resident of Switzerland, was being invited 'to apply for citizenship' of the country he once ruled. The King accepted this 'with cautious satisfaction', but saw it as only a first step. And should he be reinstated, he declared that he wanted to change the constitution so that his daughter Margarita becomes his heir.

Francois Prouvost/SIPA/Rex Features